My Fish Friends
by Brian Ardel

blue ocean press
tokyo - florida

Copyright © 2018 Brian Ardel

All rights reserved.

This publication may not be reproduced, stored in a retrieval system, or transmitted in any form or by any means, electronic, mechanical, photocopying, recording, or otherwise, without prior written permission of the publisher, except by a reviewer who may quote brief passages in a review to be printed in a periodical.

Published by: blue ocean press, an imprint of Aoishima Research Institute
U.S. (Main) Office
P.O. Box 510818
Punta Gorda, Florida 33951

807-36 Lions Plaza Ebisu
3-25-3 Higashi, Shibuya-ku, Tokyo, Japan 150

Email: contact@blueoceanpublications.com
URL: http://www.blueoceanpublications.com

ISBN: 978-4-902837-56-8

As I walked beside the sea,
the ocean's waves called out to me.
If adventure and fun is what you wish,
dive in and meet my friends the fish!
I put on my fins, I put on my mask,
I started my aquatic task.
The first fish friend that came my way,
was a gigantic manta ray.

Don't be afraid, he laughed at me,
I only eat plankton, its yummy!

A Black Angelfish looked me up and down.
He made a snort and began to frown.

I am a fish, my name is Roy.
Do you need a tour? Are you lost young boy?

The Parrotfish smiled when he saw me,
welcome to our world under the sea.

Roy took me all around the reef,
the brown Coney had a lot of teeth!

The Durgeon was electric blue.
She was quite a beauty too!

The Hawkfish face had lots of spots,
pretty orange polka dots.

The Parrotfish was powder blue.
He had a friendly smile too.

The little Blenny's name was Fred,
he chewed upon something red.

The Rock Beauty's face had quite a smile.
She swam beside me for a while.

A grumpy Coney was white and brown,
his face was stuck in a tight frown.

The Butterflyfish was yellow and white,
I think I gave him quite a fright.

The Queen Triggerfish was really cute.
She wore a brown and purple suit.

The Pufferfish was small in size,
but she sure had some pretty eyes.

The red Squirrelfish became my friend,
I didn't want my dive to end.

The Grouper had bright blue eyes, they stared at me in deep surprise.

The Hermit Crab's eyes were green,
His legs the reddest I have seen.

All good things have to end,
So said Roy, my fishy friend.
He and the Razorfish took me to shore,
I wanted to stay and swim some more.
The Razorfish smiled, "We'll see you soon!
Tomorrow we will swim at noon!"

www.ingramcontent.com/pod-product-compliance
Lightning Source LLC
Chambersburg PA
CBHW041406010526
44107CB00015B/1087